Getting Equipped To Stop Bullying:

A Kid's Survival Kit for Understanding and Coping with Violence in the Schools

by

Becki H. Boatwright, Ph.D., LPC
Counselor/Psychotherapist
Chesterfield County School District
Summit Counseling and Consulting
Patrick, SC

Teresea A. Mathis, Ed.S., LMSW
Counselor
Columbia, SC

Susan J. Smith-Rex, Ed.D.
Professor of Special Education
College of Education, Winthrop University
Rock Hill, SC

Illustrations coordinated by Ruth Ann Jackson and Kimberly Grant
Cover drawing by Michael Cooney

Copyright 1998

Educational Media Corporation®
P.O. Box 21311
Minneapolis, MN 55421-0311

(763) 781-0088 or (800) 966-3382

www.**educationalmedia**.com

ISBN 0-932796-84-2

Library of Congress Catalog No. 98-74456

Printing (Last Digit)

9   8   7   6   5   4   3   2

Production editor—

Don L. Sorenson, Ph.D.

Graphic Design—

Earl Sorenson

Illustrators—

Anthony Brice	Jamie Busby	Bernie Cooke
Michael Cooney	Margaret Cunningham	Jamie Edwards
Chris Gervais	Angela Jordan	Michael Ledford
Daniel Lee	Robbie Leslie	Jill Litherland
Jay Matthews	Beau Myers	Holly Schmidt
Justin Smith	Stanton Stebbins	Gus Williams
Sara Wingate		

Becki Boatwright, Ph.D., LPC; Teresea Mathis, Ed.S, LMSW; and Susan Smith-Rex, Ed.D.

Table of Contents

Note to Parents and Health Professionals:

There are many times when children feel unsafe. There are times when children don't feel safe enough to share their feelings with anyone. There are times when children are being BULLIED. There are times when children are involved in or aware of school violence. These are the times of which we are concerned.

As long time educators and counselors, we believe BULLYING is the basis of many life problems, i.e., low self-esteem, abuse, and violence. Our goal in this program is to provide an understanding of the dynamics of bullying and to empower children to recognize and deal with bullies at a young age in order to alleviate the possible development of problems stemming from being bullied.

The first part of this book is intended to help both bullies and victims deal with bullying and school violence. The book was carefully written to be user friendly for children. The vocabulary, illustrations, and limited number of words on each page should be inviting and helpful to children in understanding bullying and school violence.

Children have the ability to work out problems in their own lives. The second part of this book focuses on some practical ideas victims and bullies can use to get equipped to stop bullying. This section is interactive in nature. The student selects areas of concern and does the activities which will help him or her explore what needs to be done to stop bullying and school violence. Mental health projects are provided that are practical and thought provoking.

The third part of this book has practical ideas for adults to use while working with students to help them get equipped to stop bullying and school violence. Adult support, time, and attention goes a long way.

While this book can be used independently by elementary and middle school students, we highly recommend parents and mental health professionals read and discuss this book with children. In this way, the information and suggestions can be fully discussed and the children are encouraged to follow through on the strategies provided. Best wishes as you put this book to good use!

Becki H. Boatwright, Ph.D., LPC
Teresea A. Mathis, Ed.S, LMSW
Susan J. Smith-Rex, Ed.D.

Part I

Helping Children Understand Bullies and Victims

Jay Matthews

Most people have heard the word "bully." Most of us know a few people who we would call bullies.

Becki Boatwright, Ph.D., LPC; Teresea Mathis, Ed.S, LMSW; and Susan Smith-Rex, Ed.D.

Angela Jordan

Being a bully is not something of which to be proud. Usually bullies are not well liked and they can sometimes cause fear in others.

Stanton Stebbins

Usually we think bullies are boys, but that is not always true. Girls, also, are guilty of being bullies and making others feel uncomfortable.

Justin Smith

A bully is someone who abuses another person. Abuse means any bad treatment which makes a person feel sad, scared, or sick.

Chris Gervais

Bullying behavior can be shown in many ways. Usually we think of it as hitting or shoving. However, bullies can also say hurtful things in a sarcastic manner, use scary gestures, or not let another be a part of the group.

Ways to Bully

Physical	*Verbal*	*Non-Verbal*	*Isolation*
Fighting	Blaming	Being irresponsible	Ignoring
Hitting	Bossing	Finger gestures	Not listening
Kicking	Bringing up the past	Getting even	Excluding from
Punching	Intimidating	Ignoring	peer group
Pushing	Joking	Making faces	
Shoving	Making excuses	Making fists	
Slapping	Name calling	Rumors	
Stealing	Nasty statements	Sneering	
Using weapons	Put downs	Stealing	
	Sarcasm	Using scary gestures	
	Saying hurtful things	Vandalism	
	Teasing		
	Taunting		
	Threatening		

What can you add to this list?

Gus Williams

The person who is being bullied is called a victim. A victim is usually an innocent person who has done nothing to deserve the abuse. Victims should not keep the problem a secret. The only way to stop bullying is to look for ways to end it.

Ways to Stop Bullying

1. *Two is company; travel with friends.*

2. *Stay away from places bullies hang out.*

3. *Make like a banana and split. It is better to avoid a fight by walking away with dignity.*

4. *Head for a crowded place.*

5. *Talk to people you trust—parents, teachers, and friends—about how to deal with a bully.*

6. *Go ahead and make my day! Practice acting confident—how you will talk and act the next time someone bothers you.*

7. *Try ignoring the bully. If the person continues to bother you, say firmly "Cut it out!"*

8. *Participate in activities where you are likely to excel. Focus on what you do well.*

9. *Socialize with other students and try to make friends. Mix in rather than be left out.*

Margaret Cunningham

Bullying happens too often in schools, homes, and neighborhoods. School violence is increasing and everyone is concerned. Sometimes school violence is caused by bullies. However, sometimes school violence is caused by frightened and angry victims. Having some information about the bullying problem hopefully will make it less of a problem.

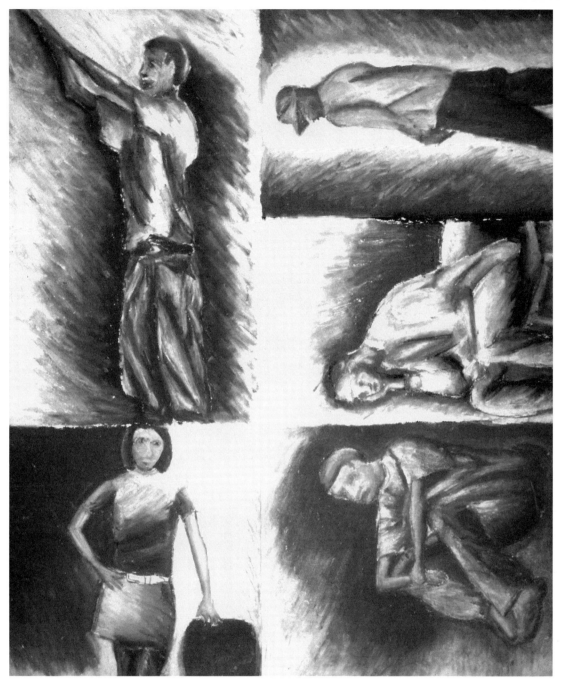

Jill Litherland

How common is the problem? One out of every seven children is either a victim or a bully—about 15% of the school population in the United States. Also, 15% of all school absenteeism is directly related to fears of being bullied at school.

Jamie Edwards

Both the victims and the bullies need help. Let's look at the victim first. Victims are usually fearful and angry when they are forced to be around a bully. They also feel nervous, shy, or lonely. Victims may cry, want to be alone, or feel a need to get back at the bully.

Michael Ledford

Victims also may feel sick and not want to go to school. Victims may not be able to concentrate on their school work and their grades may drop. This problem often causes children to have a low self-esteem. People with low self-esteem are not proud of themselves.

Beau Myers

Victims must learn how to be ASSERTIVE. They must let others know how they feel or what they need in a positive way. Bullies are not assertive; they are AGGRESSIVE. This is not good. Being aggressive means taking advantage of someone in a negative or bad way.

Anthony Brice

Later in this book you will learn some ways to become more assertive. You also will learn to identify people to whom you can turn if you need help. These helpful people belong to your support system. Together you can work to stop bullying and feel good about yourself.

Stanton Stebbins

Bullies need help as well. Bullies often are underachievers and are five times more likely than other children to fall into deeper trouble, such as traffic violations, alcohol or drug abuse, and the abuse of others.

Jamie Busby

STOOGES are persons who follow after bullies and do what they are told, even if it is wrong. BYSTANDERS watch events take place, but they are not involved. When you hear or see something that indicates something bad might happen, you should tell an adult in your support system. Possibly the event can be stopped! It is better to be safe than sorry.

Justin Smith

If you grow up seeing bullies treat others unfairly, you may think it is okay for you to do the same. It is NOT okay. We must find other ways to feel good about ourselves and to handle anger.

Jamie Edwards

Violence in television shows, movies, video games, and music often lead us to believe that bullying and aggression means power and respect. Don't forget that what you watch and hear is mostly make believe. Once you hurt someone, you can't take your actions back.

Jamie Edwards

Bernie Cooke

Parents, teachers, and others set rules to govern our behavior—to give us boundaries—and keep us safe.

Here are some examples of rules for school and home.

School Behavior Rules:

1. *We want to respect other people's space.*
2. *We want to use caring communications.*
3. *We want to include everyone when we do group activities.*
4. *We want to have a friendly class, and help other students if they are bullied.*

Home Behavior Rules:

Show respect for yourself and family by:
1. *Watching the tone of your voice.*
2. *Following your curfew.*
3. *Doing your share of the family chores without coaxing.*
4. *Following morning, bedtime, and homework routines.*
5. *Limiting TV viewing.*

Would you like to add other rules?

_____

_____

What are some rules in your home and school?

_____

_____

_____

_____

Daniel Lee

Where and when in the school or neighborhood will bullying most likely take place? Bullies usually pick the places and times where there is less adult supervision. (Halls, restrooms, playgrounds, the cafeteria, and buses).

Chris Gervais

Adults can't be everywhere all the time. Students need to learn how to look for bullying and to use ASSERTIVE leadership skills to help stop it. Many bully problems can actually be solved by students, as long as calm, assertive talking takes place.

Holly Schmidt

Adults need to help students to develop rules against bullying. Together they must believe that bullies have no right to be in charge. All students should feel safe and comfortable at school, in their homes, and in their neighborhoods.

Becki Boatwright, Ph.D., LPC; Teresea Mathis, Ed.S, LMSW; and Susan Smith-Rex, Ed.D.

Sara Wingate

By being more aware of the bully problem and by having high expectations of all students, our schools and neighborhoods can be safer.

Getting Equipped to Stop Bullying

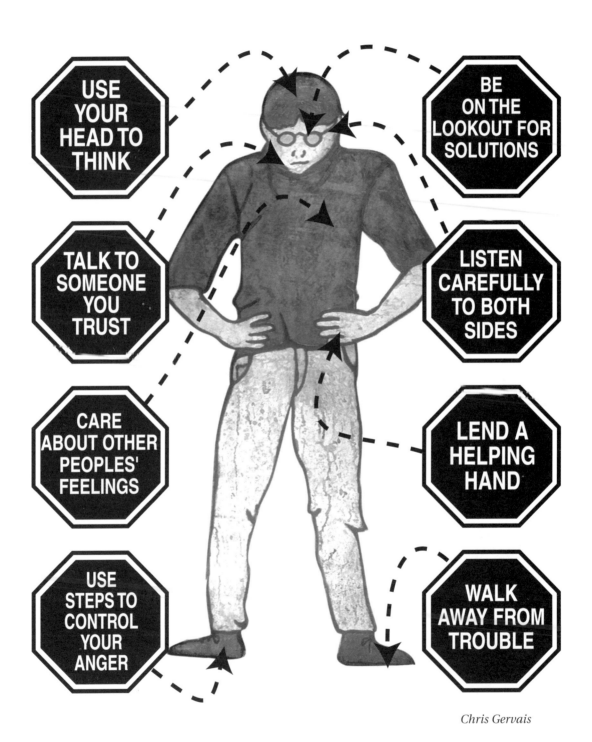

USE YOUR HEAD TO THINK

BE ON THE LOOKOUT FOR SOLUTIONS

TALK TO SOMEONE YOU TRUST

LISTEN CAREFULLY TO BOTH SIDES

CARE ABOUT OTHER PEOPLES' FEELINGS

LEND A HELPING HAND

USE STEPS TO CONTROL YOUR ANGER

WALK AWAY FROM TROUBLE

Chris Gervais

Becki Boatwright, Ph.D., LPC; Teresea Mathis, Ed.S, LMSW; and Susan Smith-Rex, Ed.D.

Part II

Practical Ideas for Victims and Bullies to Get Equipped to Stop Bullying

Bullying affects the bully, the victim, and the bystander. Here are some ideas to help you to better understand and cope with bullying. Think about which ones you may need help with in order to get equipped to stop bullying, then turn to the appropriate page.

1. **Bullies, Victims, and Bystanders** (Introduction)

   Learning the facts about bullies, victims, and bystanders.

2. **Behavior and Self-Control** (Self-Monitoring and Anger Management)

   Learning self-control and ways to handle anger positively.

3. **Standing Up for Myself** (Assertiveness Training)

   Learning to act confident and plan ahead.

4. **Getting Along with Others** (Social Training)

   Learning to make friends and get along with others.

5. **To Whom Do You Go to for Help?** (Support Systems)

   Learning to identify helpful people and seek help.

Terms

Abuse	To treat in a wrong or hurtful way.
Aggressive	Negatively taking advantage of someone for no reason.
Anger Management	Handle anger positively so it goes away without hurting anyone.
Assertive	Positively let others know your feelings; act confident; get help.
Anxiety	A feeling of fearful uneasiness or worry about what may happen.
Bully	Someone who hurts a person who is weaker or at a disadvantage.
Bystander	Someone who watches an event take place, but is not involved.
Coping Skills	Positive ways to act to feel good about yourself and solve problems.
Defenses	Walls we create to hide feelings: joking, daydreaming, talking back, and acting out.
Leadership Training:	Summer program to train "Peace Patrols" and "Peer Mediators" in mediation skills
Negative Actions	Hurtful behavior.
Direct Bullying	Attacks on a person.
Physical	Hit, slap, push, kick.
Verbal	Nasty statements.
Non-Verbal	Making faces, ignoring, making fists, finger gestures.
Indirect Bullying	To leave someone out of the group.
Isolation	To separate someone from the group.
Passive	Giving in to a bully's demand.
Peace Patrol	A student who patrols areas to keep others safe.
Peer Mediator	A student who helps referred students find positive solutions to their conflicts.
Poor self-esteem	When a person feels of little or no worth.
Strategy	A careful plan for achieving a goal.
Stooge	A person who follows a bully and does what he or she is told, even if it is wrong.
Support System	People you know to whom you can turn for help or advice.
Vandalism	The willful destruction of property.
Victim	Person cheated, fooled, or injured through hurtful behaviors.
Violent	Extremely forceful behavior which shows strong negative feelings.

Pre/Post Questionnaire

Part I: Circle the word you choose.

1. Which term describes someone who purposely hurts another person's feelings or body?

   Victim   Friend   Bully   Stranger

2. If you let someone in your support system know about a problem bothering you, you are:

   Aggressive   Assertive   Talkative   Passive

3. A person who is injured, cheated, made fun of, or ignored is called a:

   Victim   Friend   Bully   Stranger

4. Which type of bullying bothers you most?

   Punching   Teasing   Being ignored   Being bossy

Part II: Circle yes or no.

5. Have you ever been a victim of someone bullying you?   Yes   No

6. If you've been a victim, did you tell your teacher?   Yes   No

7. If you've been a victim, did you tell your parents?   Yes   No

8. Have you ever injured, cheated, or made fun of someone?   Yes   No

9. Do you think teachers at your school do a good job of monitoring students' behavior during lunch and recess?   Yes   No

10. Do you admire or like bullies?   Yes   No

11. Do you think bullying is a problem in your school?   Yes   No

12. If bullying could be stopped at your school, would you like school better?   Yes   No

13. If everyone helped stop bullying, would you be willing to help by reporting problems to your teacher?   Yes   No

14. Should the victim walk away from a bully to keep peace?   Yes   No

15. Should the victim use a firm, convincing tone of voice and tell the bully to "cut it out"?   Yes   No

Pre/Post Questionnaire Results

Total number in class: _____

Part I: Write the number of students who chose each answer.

1. Victim _____   Friend _____   Bully _____   Stranger _____

2. Aggressive _____   Assertive _____   Talkative _____   Passive _____

3. Victim _____   Friend _____   Bully _____   Stranger _____

4. Punching _____   Teasing _____   Being ignored _____   Bossing _____

Part II: Write the number of students who responded each way.

5.   Yes _____   No _____

6.   Yes _____   No _____

7.   Yes _____   No _____

8.   Yes _____   No _____

9.   Yes _____   No _____

10.   Yes _____   No _____

11.   Yes _____   No _____

12.   Yes _____   No _____

13.   Yes _____   No _____

14.   Yes _____   No _____

15.   Yes _____   No _____

Learning the Facts About Bullying

1. School bullying is a significant problem! One in seven students is either a bully or victim. Fifty-six percent of students have personally witnessed (bystander) some type of bullying at school and 71% report incidents of bullying at their school.

2. *Direct* bullying may be teasing, taunting, threatening, hitting, and stealing. *Indirect* bullying may be intentionally isolating a student or spreading rumors.

3. Boys typically engage in direct bullying and girls engage in indirect bullying. Students who bully seem to need to feel powerful and in control.

4. Bullies acquire aggressive habits through biological (temperament, physique) and environmental (family, peers, media) factors. Sixty percent of those characterized as bullies in grades six to nine had at least one criminal conviction by age 24.

5. Fear and suffering are part of the everyday lives of victims. They are more often anxious, insecure, cautious, sensitive, shy, lonely, withdrawn, or cry easily.

6. Fifteen percent of all school absenteeism is directly related to fears of being bullied at school.

7. There are things victims can do to prevent bullying (use one's support system, learn assertiveness skills, use peer mediation).

8. Forty-three percent of students try to help the victim; 33% said they should help but do not.

9. Bullying tends to be at its peak during the middle school years.

10. Schools that have implemented programs report a 50% reduction in bullying. To be effective, the program must involve the whole school-community.

11. School violence is increasing. Over 50% of US public schools have experienced at least one crime incident. Ten percent of all public schools have experienced violent crimes that were reported to law enforcement. (Sixty-three percent of children ages 7 to 10 worry that they may die young.)

12. Thirty-one percent of public school students report gangs in their schools.

13. One out of twenty students has seen a student with a gun at school. (6,093 students were expelled from public schools last year for bringing a fire arm to school; 9% of all expulsions occurred in elementary schools.)

14. During the school year 1996-97, there were 190,000 physical attacks without a weapon, 116,000 incidents of theft or larceny, 4,000 incidents of rape or sexual battery, and 11,000 incidents of physical attacks with a weapon.

    Education Week, Aug/Sep 1997; *ERIC Digest* 1997; National Center for Education Statistics, 1998 Bureau of Justice Statistics; *Time,* May 18, 1998.

1. Bullies, Victims, and Bystanders

The goals of our program are:

A. Increase awareness of the bullying problem and how it relates to school violence.

B. Motivate parents, teachers, administrators, and students to become more involved in intervening in possible bullying situations in order to decrease school violence.

C. Develop clear rules against bullying behavior.

D. Provide support and protection for the victim.

The objectives of our program follow.

Students will be able to:

A. Define and recognize bullying.

B. Practice strategies for dealing with bullying.

C. Follow school rules against bullying.

D. Contribute towards making the school environment more inviting for everyone.

Bullies, Victims and Bystanders—A Closer Look

Bullies	Victims	Bystanders
Common Characteristics	**Common Characteristics**	**Common Characteristics**
want power	often develop low self-esteem	affected
feel hurt inside	feel isolated; cry easily	feel powerless to do anything
lack social skills	lack social skills	scared
use others to get what they want	grades may suffer	learn to manage the lowered self-esteem and loss of control that accompanies feelings of not being safe and inability to take action
problems with seeing things from someone else's view/ perspective	singled out because of being shy, sensitive, anxious, or insecure	
concerned with their own pleasure, not thinking of others	may turn to ways to protect themselves or seek revenge	
Extrovert: outgoing, aggressive, active, expressive, often end up in trouble as adults; angry & mean on the surface; get their way by force or harassment; may feel inferior, insecure, and unsure of themselves; reject rules and regulations to feel superior	may be overweight, physically small, having a disability, or of a different race or religious faith	Can help stop victims from being bullied by: • speaking up when someone is being bullied. • creating a distraction. • looking for a Peace Patrol. • getting an adult to help.
Introvert: try to control by smooth-talking, saying the "right" things at the "right" time		

	Areas of Need	
• self-monitoring	• self-monitoring	
• social training	• social training	• social training
• support systems	• support systems	• support systems
• anger management training	• anger management training	
	• assertiveness training	• assertiveness training

Bullying can have a lasting effect on everyone involved—bullies, victims and bystanders. There are many steps you can take to deal with the problem of bullying. Your first step is to recognize the serious consequences and commit yourself to do all you can to stop it. Bullies and victims share many of the same desperate feelings and pressures. It is important to protect victims of bullying as well as to be sensitive and committed to helping bullies change their behavior.

2. Behavior and Self-Control
A. Self-monitoring

1. Using the right equipment—Your head and your heart are two of the best tools you have to help you monitor yourself and keep yourself under control. Use your head to stop and think about making good decisions. Your heart can be your vehicle to caring about other people's feelings as well as your own.

   STOP, think and ask yourself three questions before doing **anything** else:

   1. What am I getting ready to do?
   2. What will happen if I do this?
   3. What can I do instead?

   (Make yourself a card to remember these.)

2. The "Right" Signals—Bullies, victims, and bystanders develop low self-esteem at one time or another. The truth is that we all have times when we feel a loss of control or not "real good" about ourselves. What is important is that we learn to give ourselves the "right" or positive signals to help ourselves feel better. It's called "self-talk." To feel better about ourselves, it's important to think good thoughts. Do your best and learn to like yourself. Be your own coach and encourage yourself. Try an experiment for one week. Each time something in your thoughts causes you to feel bad about yourself, give yourself a good talking to and change those signals to positive ones.

   Practice signals like: "I'll do my best."   "I'm all right."

                                 "I'm going to try."   "I'm doing fine."

   Now think of three "right" signals you can give yourself. Find things you do well and enjoy.

   1. _____   4. _____
   2. _____   5. _____
   3. _____   6. _____

3. Keeping on Track—Charting. Talk with your teachers, parents, and/or counselor about helping you with this project. On the following chart, write the class rules and personal goals you want to work on improving daily. **Stick to it.** At the end of each class have your teacher rate your behavior; then, at the end of the day, rate yourself. Have an agreed number of points you need to earn rewards (playtime, TV time, time with friends, etc.). Keep a calendar in a special place at home to remind yourself of the great days you are having. Put a plus, star, smiley face, or something special on the calendar for each "good" day: don't put anything on the days that need extra work. Remember to focus on your goals and the positives.

Name _____ Date _____

Grading Scale: 4= Excellent 3= Good 2=Fair 1=Poor					
Class Rules	**My Score**				
	Math	Language Arts	Science SS	Related Arts	Self
1. I will have a good attitude.					
2. I will be respectful to others.					
3. I will _____					
4. I will _____					
5. I will _____					
Personal Goals	**My Score**				
1. _____					
2. _____					

Teacher Comments: _____

_____

_____

Parent Comments: _____

_____

Parent Signature: _____

Six Steps to Learning Self-Control

_____ 1. Recognize when you are too excited and can't focus your attention.

_____ 2. Think of three alternative choices before you make a decision.

_____ 3. Talk about your feelings when something bothers you. (Use your support system.)

_____ 4. Listen carefully to what other people are saying.

_____ 5. Respect other people's space. Pretend everyone has a hoop around them and you can't get closer than that hoop.

_____ 6. Use self-talk. Be your own coach and encourage yourself to try harder!

Even the best equipment has to go into the shop for maintenance and repairs. Think of this as your trip to the Service Center. Examples of two different service forms are listed below. Make copies of the blank form below so you can make your own service forms. (Tape one inside your notebook and another on your bathroom mirror to help you feel more self-control.)

Name _____ Date _____

1. Am I using eye contact?
2. Did I walk with confidence?
3. Did I speak up?
4. Did I use *self-talk*?

Name _____ Date _____

1. Am I staying calm?
2. Did I stop and think?
3. Did I walk away?
4. Did I find a place to relax and think?

Make up your own service form. What repairs do you need to work on?

Name _____ Date _____

1. _____
2. _____
3. _____
4. _____

B. Anger Management

One of the strongest emotions is anger. Anger is an okay feeling to have, but how you handle anger is important. Some rules you need to remember are:

You will not hurt yourself.

You will not hurt someone else.

You will not damage property.

Sometimes holding your feelings in hurts you. If you carry your angry feelings around inside, these feelings can interfere with life. It is important to get these feelings out in a positive way. Here are some things you can do:

Count to ten, or higher if you need to.

Talk to someone you trust.

Bounce a ball or choose other outside activities.

Listen to music.

Write down your angry feelings.

Self-talk: Stop, take a breath—calm down—keep calm.

Leave the scene and do something relaxing (nap, TV, walk).

Do something for someone else.

Read a good book.

REMEMBER: No negative talk—don't take it out on someone else.

List three things you can do to help when you're angry.

1. _____

2. _____

3. _____

Use steps to control your anger

Step 1. Be aware: Be aware of signs that you're getting angry.

Step 2. Stop and calm down: Take some deep breaths. Give yourself some time to cool down and sort out what's wrong and what you are really feeling.

Step 3. Think: Think about what happens when you get angry, blow up, or keep it inside:

- Anger gets me in trouble.
- I often get into a fight when I'm angry.
- Other people get mad at me because of what I say or do.
- I don't always know how I will act when I'm angry.
- I get embarrassed because of what I do or say when I'm angry.

Step 4.Check out choices and consequences: Think about the choices you have for handling your anger and the consequences of each choice.

- What will happen if I lose my temper?
- Should I stay, walk away, or ignore it?

Step 5.Decide and Do It: *Decide* which choice is best for everyone and *do* it.

C_2 = CALM AND COOL

Here are twelve examples of *calming* thoughts to say to yourself to help you keep your *cool* when you are angry.

1. I won't get myself in trouble.
2. I *can* control my temper.
3. It's not worth getting angry.
4. I won't make such a big deal about this.
5. I'm not going to let this get to me.
6. I can't expect people to act the way I want.
7. I'll use humor and make a joke of the situation.

Robbie Leslie

8. She wants me to get angry. Well, I won't give her the satisfaction. She will just be disappointed.
9. I don't have to prove myself.
10. As long as I keep cool, I'm in control of things.
11. I'll grow up and not blow up.
12. I won't be made to look like a fool; I'll just keep my cool.

Talk things over. Talk to someone you trust who will support your staying out of trouble (a *real* friend, a teacher, a counselor, a parent, etc.). After you are calm and cool, talk to the person with whom you are angry.

- Tell what you're mad about.
- Tell what you want to happen.
- Find someone to help the two of you talk things out.

Step 6. Feel good! Let go of any anger that may be left behind by:

- Doing something active.
- Doing something you really enjoy.
- Getting exercise.
- Trying to forgive and forget; put it behind you.
- Giving yourself a pat on the back; a compliment.
- Treating yourself to some fun with a friend.

C. Working the "bugs" out

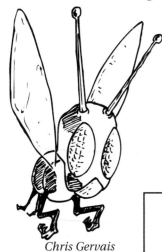

Chris Gervais

Knowing what "bugs" or bothers you and causes you to get angry can help you find ways to stay calm and keep self-control. Below, write something that someone does that really "bugs" you. Then write a "calm down," —something you can say to help yourself stay calm and cool; or an "I" message you can say to the one who's bugging you. An "I" message would be:

- "**What** is bothering you?"
- "**Why** is it bothering you?"
- "**How** would you like things to change?"

> It "bugs" me when someone takes ***food out of my lunch bag.***
>
> I can calm down by thinking or saying *"I don't like it when you touch my things without asking. Please **don't do it anymore.**"*

Try filling in the next examples:

> It "bugs" me when _____
>
> I can calm down by thinking or saying _____

> It "bugs" me when _____
>
> I can calm down by thinking or saying _____

Think about and describe a person you know who handles anger in a positive way or interview an adult in your school for ideas to handle anger in a positive way. Keep a diary for a week while you practice keeping your cool. Remember to compliment yourself on a job well done.

1. After you have done something to help control your anger, say things to yourself like:
   - "I was smart enough to walk away."
   - "I am glad I remembered to imagine a stop sign."
   - "I used an "I" message without being mean or insulting."

2. Tell yourself how good you feel about doing the right thing. You could say:
   - "I handled that pretty well."
   - "I'm doing better all the time."
   - "I'm growing up."
   - "I have good control."

3. Do the same thing next time you start to get angry; know how much better you will feel.

3. Standing Up for Myself

A. You too can be assertive

Being assertive means acting confident and letting others know your feelings in positive ways. Don't let yourself be a victim. There *are* things *you* can do.

Step One: Think Assertive

The first thing you need to do is to think and use your head. Size up the person and the situation.

Are you alone?

Is this person dangerous?

Is this person out to hurt you?

Does this person have a weapon?

Is this person using drugs or alcohol?

If the answer to *any* of these questions is yes, walk away with dignity. Walk in the direction of a friend or an adult. Head for a crowded place and get help.

Step Two: Look Assertive

Keep calm and cool! Watch your body language. Your body language sends out important signals about how you are feeling. Keep your head up and your posture straight. Focus on where you are going, and walk like you have somewhere to go. You could even check your watch, as if you have somewhere important to be at a specific time.

Step Three: Act Assertive

1. If the bully does not seem dangerous, try ignoring the bully and going on your way.

2. If the person continues to bother you, say firmly, "Leave me alone," or "Cut it out."

3. Being in control of yourself can help you get control of the situation. Talk with people you trust about how to deal with a bully.

4. Practice acting confident—how you will talk and act if someone bothers you.

5. Being assertive can stop bullying. Review page 13, "Ways to Stop Bullying."

B. Be on the *Look Out* for Solutions:

1. Ask your teacher to make a *Bully Box* using the following *Situation Cards.* You can also make your own cards by writing a description of any bully problem.

2. In groups of three, fill out the situation cards and discuss anything new in the *Bully Box.*

Situation 1: Jenny has just moved into the area and hates school. She eats by herself every day and at recess usually stands near the door wishing the bell would ring. Step 1: Define the problem: _____ Step 2: List 3 solutions 1. _____ 　　　　　　　　　　　　2. _____ 　　　　　　　　　　　　3. _____ Step 3: Choose the best solution. _____ Step 4: Evaluate the solution. _____	Situation 4: _____ _____ _____ _____ Step 1: Define the problem: _____ Step 2: List 3 solutions 1. _____ 　　　　　　　　　　　　2. _____ 　　　　　　　　　　　　3. _____ Step 3: Choose the best solution. _____ Step 4: Evaluate the solution. _____
Situation 2: Tommy wants to buy ice cream every day. If he doesn't have enough money, all he needs to do is tell one of the first grade students to give him a quarter and his problem is solved. Step 1: Define the problem: _____ Step 2: List 3 solutions 1. _____ 　　　　　　　　　　　　2. _____ 　　　　　　　　　　　　3. _____ Step 3: Choose the best solution. _____ Step 4: Evaluate the solution. _____	Situation 5: _____ _____ _____ _____ _____ Step 1: Define the problem: _____ Step 2: List 3 solutions 1. _____ 　　　　　　　　　　　　2. _____ 　　　　　　　　　　　　3. _____ Step 3: Choose the best solution. _____ Step 4: Evaluate the solution. _____
Situation 3: Billy's headaches are getting worse. He hasn't liked school since Brad moved into their town. Brad has thrown Billy's books out the window three times. Step 1: Define the problem: _____ Step 2: List 3 solutions 1. _____ 　　　　　　　　　　　　2. _____ 　　　　　　　　　　　　3. _____ Step 3: Choose the best solution. _____ Step 4: Evaluate the solution. _____	Situation 6: _____ _____ _____ _____ Step 1: Define the problem: _____ Step 2: List 3 solutions 1. _____ 　　　　　　　　　　　　2. _____ 　　　　　　　　　　　　3. _____ Step 3: Choose the best solution. _____ Step 4: Evaluate the solution. _____

4. Getting Along with Others

Often, bullies and victims don't have many true friends because they don't know how to make friends or be good friends. When bullies have positive friendships they have less need to be bullies. When victims have friends they feel less lonely and it is more difficult to bully someone with friends. The *Friendship Model* has *four* basic steps, which can help you make friends and keep friends.

Friendship Model	
Steps	**What to Do**
1. CHECK IT OUT	Think good thoughts about yourself. Use clear messages. Stop muddy messages. Look at how others are acting and what you have in common.
2. REACH OUT	Give compliments. Example: "I really like your hair." Use everyday statements. Example: "What is your favorite band?"
3. TRY IT OUT	Talk to yourself. Does it feel right? Is it working? Is this group worth the effort?
4. WORK IT OUT	NOT WORKING—Take a *time out*. Check yourself out again. WORKING—Be sensitive, trustworthy, share thoughts and feelings.

Clear messages can be sent in different ways. One way to give clear messages is to use "I" messages. Here's how it works:

"I" Message

I FEEL (State your feeling) ____irritated_____

WHEN YOU (State your specific behavior) ____keep making fun of my glasses_____

BECAUSE (State the effect on your life) _____it embarrasses me_____

AND I WANT (Say what you need to make the situation better) ___you to stop doing it

---

Let's try it. Think of something you feel strongly about. This can be a good feeling or a bad feeling. However, practice saying your "I" message calmly.

I FEEL _____

WHEN YOU _____

BECAUSE _____

AND I WANT _____

Now that you know how to make friends, you should know that sometimes you will have conflicts with your friends. Sometimes you just don't agree or see things the same way because you are both individuals. This doesn't mean one of you is wrong and one is right; both can be right. The trick is to be able to solve the conflict without losing the friendship. Sometimes you'll need to BREAK to resolve the conflict in a friendly way.

BREAK Conflict Formula

Be a friend.

Remember to use your head and think.

Evaluate the conflict or problem.

Agree you want to work it out.

Keep working until you find a solution.

Be willing to compromise.

Who is the conflict with, what is it about, your part in it?

What can you do differently next time?

Ask about the other person's feelings.

"I" message to tell your side; listen to the other side.

Dealing with someone else's anger can be difficult. Sometimes another person is angry with you when you may not be angry. Or, you may feel that person should not be angry. You can always use the **BREAK** conflict formula when this happens. However, here are some more ideas that may help.

- Keep calm.

- Ask what is wrong. Then, listen.

- Try to understand the other person's point of view.

- Explain your side of the story.

- Apologize.

- Brainstorm ways to solve the problem.

- Ask for help from an adult.

- Take a **BREAK** or *time out* in the office to cool off.

You may have some other ideas. Think about it. You can put them here:

_____

_____

_____

_____

Here are three helpful cards to be copied for students to have available.

BREAK Card:

The first letter of these sentences spells BREAK. Carry this card with you as a reminder of a way to work out conflicts and get along with others.

BREAK Card

Be a friend.

Remember to use your head and think.

Evaluate the conflict or problem.

Agree you want to work it out.

Keep working until you find a solution.

SELF-CONTROL Card:

This card will help you take control of your actions so you can stop conflict before it happens. There are three questions on the stop sign to encourage you to stop and think before acting.

SELF-CONTROL Card

1. What am I getting ready to do?

2. What will happen if I do this?

3. What can I do instead?

ESCAPE Card:

This card is for when you need to take a BREAK to cool off and think things over. Use this card as a pass to the office or to see the counselor.

ESCAPE Card

I need a BREAK!

5. To Whom Do You Go to for Help?

In your school, there is likely a support group for students who are bullies, victims, or bystanders. Ask your counselor or a teacher for information about small group counseling. Support groups help you to see that you are not the only one dealing with the problem. Many kids your age meet to encourage each other and to discuss ideas for coping. The group offers a safe place for you to discuss your feelings and to enjoy being with others.

Just as important as a support group, are the individuals with whom you feel comfortable discussing your situation. Your school counselor and other trusted adults can be counted on to be helpful. It is a good idea to build a network of caring people, both adults and students. Trusted adults may include a parent, coach, teacher, counselor, best friend's mother, religious leader, and so forth. Below, you can place persons in your support group on the circles. On the next page you can make a list of people who can offer support. There is also a letter to fill out if you need help from your counselor. (See page 52.)

Friendships with peers may grow out of support groups and other activities in which you participate. Clubs and after school activities are a good way to develop friendships and to focus on good things that will help you to move along with life.

What does your support team look like? Fill in as many circles as possible. Be sure to include individuals and groups who are helpful to you. Remember, you don't have to be the "Lone Ranger." There are many people who care. You can develop your support team as large as you would like. It seems to gradually grow as you reach out.

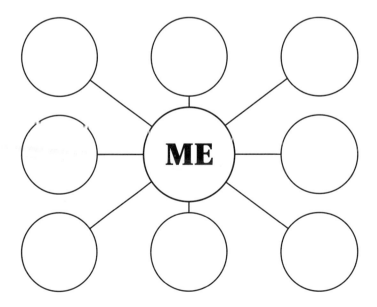

INDIVIDUALS and GROUPS that Make Up My Support Team

Write names and telephone numbers of people you would like to have in your support system.

	Name	Telephone Number
Friends:		
Family Members:		
School Personnel:		
Com. Agencies:		
Others:		

Dear Counselor,

I am writing this letter because (Write the problem that is bothering you.) _____

_____

_____

_____

_____

The problem is bothering me in the following ways: _____

_____

_____

I think I can solve the problem by (List at least two ways you could help solve the problem.) _____

_____

_____

PROBLEM AREAS (Can be used in completing this form.)

1. Feel left out a lot; feel sad and lonely

2. Need more friends; don't feel good about myself

3. Don't get along well with others

4. Someone is bothering or bullying me

5. Family concerns

6. Grades are low

7. Don't know how to study

8. Bored

I would like to have a conference to talk about solving this problem.

Sincerely,

_____   _____
(Your name/grade)   (Your teacher's name/date)

Part III

Practical Ideas for Adults to Help Victims and Bullies Get Equipped to Stop Bullying

When adults work together with students to establish a team effort, we can significantly decrease bullying and make home and school a more inviting, enjoyable, and motivating place to be. Here are some ideas adults can initiate to help victims and bullies *get equipped to stop bullying*.

1. Mediation Skills and Leadership Training
   (Peer Mediators and Peace Patrols)

   Learning to cultivate listening, communication, and problem-solving skills.

Turn to Page 55

2. Intervention Tools
   (Activities/suggestions for parents, schools, and communities)

   Learning to create opportunities for belonging and increasing self-esteem.

Turn to Page 72

1. Mediation Skills and Leadership Training

When students, teachers, parents, and administrators work together, we can significantly decrease bullying and make school a more inviting, enjoyable, and motivating place to be. Throughout the school year, teachers and counselors should train ALL students to have a plan for managing conflicts. An important aspect of the program's success is to have every student, in grades 3 through 8, actively involved in **observing** and **reporting** "bully" behavior. Those students who demonstrate strong leadership roles will be invited to participate in a summer leadership program. Throughout the program, students will be taught skills to serve in the roles of "Peer Mediator" or "Peace Patrol." These skills provide students with the opportunity to find positive resolutions to conflicts, and give students a way to work together.

Conflicts that **cannot** be mediated include disputes involving weapons, drugs, physical abuse, and physical altercations. Conflicts that cannot be resolved with mediation should be referred back to the administrator in charge of discipline.

It is important for students serving in these leadership roles to be trained and ready when school begins. In late April, students should be selected by their peers, teachers, and administrators to participate in the Leadership Training Program.

Important skills to be learned include:

People skills and leadership potential.

Respect of peers or ability to gain respect.

Good verbal skills.

Good listening skills.

Willingness to stay with the program for at least one year.

Ability to honor confidentiality.

The next step is to see if the nominated students would be interested and committed to participating in the training program. Meet with students prior to the end of the school year to explain that they have been chosen by their teachers and peers to serve in a leadership role in their school. Give the students the following:

1. An explanation of mediation or conflict management.
2. An application and permission slip.
3. A Conflict Manager's Commitment form.
4. A schedule of training (two days in the summer).

(All forms will be returned to the school counselor two weeks before the end of the school year.)

An Explanation of Mediation or Conflict Management:

Mediation is used to help students who are in conflict get to the bottom of the problem and help them come up with solutions. The best agreement is one that the conflicting students arrive at themselves.

Peer Mediators are called on by a school administrator or counselor to help students. These students have a choice to try mediation. When students agree to mediation, the administrator or counselor then refers them to Peer Mediators.

The mediation process is simple. Peer Mediators meet with students who are in conflict. Each student tells his or her story and how he or she feels about the problem. Mediators try to help work out bad feelings these students may have toward one another, while searching for solutions.

Mediators are not judges. They are acting as a go-between for the people in conflict. Mediators listen without placing blame. They focus on the future, rather than on what happened in the past.

In mediation everyone is a winner. Both students come away with something positive. Both compromise and both are given the chance to express their thoughts and feelings.

A word of warning—mediation may not always be successful. It may work for some and not for others. Some conflicts may need to be solved in other ways.

Leadership Application

Name _____   Grade _____

Please answer the following questions:

1. Why do you want to become a **Peer Mediator** or a member of the **Peace Patrol**? _____

   _____

2. What qualities do you have that will help you be a good conflict manager? _____

   _____

   _____

3. What type of conflicts do you think are most frequent? _____

   _____

   _____

4. List any school or community activities in which you are involved. _____

   _____

   _____

5. If selected, do you agree to attend the required two-day training session? _____

   _____

Student signature _____   Date _____

Parent signature _____   Date _____

Teacher recommendation:

I recommend _____ to be a conflict manager.

Comments: _____

   _____

   _____

Return application to _____   By _____

Congratulations!

You have been selected to participate in the Leadership Training Program at _____ School. You will receive training in mediation and conflict management skills in order to serve as a member of the **Peace Patrol** or as a **Peer Mediator**.

We are excited about the program and training. We look forward to working with you in the summer and the coming year. If your parents have any questions about this program, please have them contact _____ at _____.

Sincerely,

_____
School Administrator

Chris Gervais

_____
Counselor

I give my permission for _____ to be involved in the Leadership Training Program and to serve in this role for the _____ school year.

Parent's Signature _____ Date _____

Date Scheduled for Training: _____

Leadership Training

Day One

8:30—10:30	Introduction
	Guidelines and Ice Breaker activity (p. 56)
	A Conflict Manager is... is not (p. 60)
	Terms (p. 33); Learning the Facts (p. 36)
	Rules for Problem Solving (p. 61)
	Quick Team Building activities
10:30—10:45	Break
10:45—12:30	Be On the Look Out for Solutions (p. 46)
	Role play "I" messages (p. 47)
	Triggers and Escalators. (What pushes your anger button?)
	Feelings (pp. 62-63)
12:30— 1:00	Lunch (provided)
1:00— 2:30	Video—Sunburst Mediation Workshop (800-431-1934)
	Wrap up and end with a quick group activity.

Day Two

8:30—10:30	Review Day One
	Active listening discussion (p. 64)
	Role-plays
	Discuss roles of Peer Mediators and Peace Patrols (pp. 60, 65, 69)
10:30—10:45	Break
10:45—12:30	Break into Peer Mediator and Peace Patrol groups
	—Peer Mediators—role play the mediator's guidelines (pp. 65-66)
	—Peace Patrols—role play the Peace Patrol model (p. 69)
12:30— 1:00	Lunch (provided)
1:00— 2:00	Continue practicing role play situations.
2:00— 2:30	Closing: Conflict Manager's Commitment (p. 70)
	Certificates (p. 71), pictures

The beginning of the school year:

1. Inservice teachers.
2. Introduce Peace Patrols and Peer Mediators to students.
3. Introduce Peace Patrols and Peer Mediators to parents through newsletter and PTO.

A Conflict Manager...

IS	IS NOT
A team player	A police officer
A helping individual	A judge or juror
A person you can trust	A person who gives out orders or advice
A person who treats other students and their problems with respect	A person who gossips about other students' conflicts
An active listener	A person who interrupts or calls attention to himself/herself
A fair person (not taking sides or assigning blame)	
A dependable person	
A mediator or a Peace Patrol	

Rules For Problem Solving

1. Keep calm.

2. Agree to *try* to work out the problem.

3. Identify the problem.

4. Listen to each other with open minds.

5. Treat each other with respect.

6. Take responsibility for your actions.

7. Brainstorm ways to solve the problem.

8. Agree to solve the problem together.

Feeling Words

Afraid	Angry	Anxious
Ashamed	Awful	Bored
Brave	Caring	Cautious
Comfortable	Confident	Confused
Curious	Daring	Discouraged
Depressed	Different	Disgusted
Embarrassed	Encouraged	Enraged
Exhausted	Fearful	Frightened
Frustrated	Funny	Glad
Gloomy	Guilty	Happy
Hateful	Hysterical	Hurt
Important	Jealous	Lonely
Loved	Loving	Mad
Mean	Mixed-up	Moody
Mischievous	Nice	Overwhelmed
Patient	Puzzled	Queasy
Riled-up	Ridiculous	Rushed
Sad	Scared	Shy
Shocked	Silly	Sensitive
Special	Sympathetic	Surprised
Suspicious	Strong	Terrible
Uncomfortable	Understood	Understanding
Upset	Vicious	Wonderful
Warm	Worried	Wilted
Yucky	Young	Zaney

Learning About Feelings

1. When the teacher doesn't call on you when you know the answer, you might feel
   _____.

2. When your mother takes you shopping, you might feel_____
   _____.

3. When you are surprised on your birthday, you might feel_____
   _____.

4. When you find your favorite video game broken, you might feel_____
   _____.

5. Your friend's puppy got run over. Your friend might feel _____
   _____.

6. When you are standing in line and someone breaks in front of you, you might feel
   _____.

7. When someone pushes you and laughs, you might feel _____
   _____

8. You have food on your face after lunch. You might feel_____
   _____

9. Your best friend got an "F" on his English test. He might feel _____
   _____

10. You are elected to the Student Council. You might feel _____
    _____

   Brainstorm some other situations and discuss how you might feel.
   _____
   _____

Active Listening Steps

1. Put yourself in the other person's place to try to understand what he or she is saying and feeling.

2. Show understanding through nonverbal behaviors such as:

   Facial expressions;

   Gestures or head shake;

   Eye contact;

   Posture or body language.

3. In your own words, restate important thoughts and feelings.

4. Do *not* interrupt, give suggestions, or bring up problems from your own experience.

5. Ask relevant questions, stay on track.

6. Express support. For example say, "You seem upset about what happened."

7. Summarize the main points.

These steps can help students feel more comfortable and encouraged to continue talking

Mediator's Guidelines

The following may help you remember the steps for mediation.

Step 1. Getting Started.

It is important to start with introductions and a discussion of the rules.

Mediator 1. My name is _____ and this is _____. We are peer mediators. Please tell us your names.

It is important for you to know that peer mediators are here to help **you** find ways to solve **your** conflict. You must both agree on a solution.

Mediators do not take sides. We are not judges, and we are not here to tell you what to do. We are here to help you solve your conflict.

Your discussion is confidential. There are some exceptions. If drugs, weapons, or abuse are involved, we must report it to our advisor. We do complete a report about what has been agreed upon during mediation. (see page 67)

Mediator 2. There are some rules you must agree to follow before we get started. They are:

1. Agree you want to solve the problem/conflict.

2. Be honest.

3. Treat each other with respect.

4. Listen to each other with an open mind without interrupting.

5. Agree to come up with ways to solve the problem/conflict.

6. Agree to carry out your agreement for solving the problem/conflict.

7. Do not discuss this situation with friends after you leave mediation.

Can you agree to these rules?

Post the *Rules for Mediation* found on page 68.

Step 2. What happened?

Each mediator takes turns asking each of the students in conflict to tell his or her side of the story.

Note: It may be helpful to use questions like: What happened first? When? How? and so forth. Use the students' names. If the story gets too involved you may need to take some notes. Use *Active Listening Steps* on page 64.

Step 3. Look for possible solutions.

Each mediator asks each of the students to brainstorm ways the problem could be solved. Remind the students that these are only ideas and it is not the time to pick a solution.

Note: This can be the hardest part of mediation. You may have to ask the students to change roles and talk about how they feel the other person would like the conflict to be solved.

Mediators may need to remind the students that they agreed to come up with ways to solve this problem. Encourage students to think of more ways to solve the problem. The mediators can make suggestions in the form of questions.

Copy down each idea and then read all of the ideas.

Step 4. Select a solution.

This is the time to pick the idea or ideas you both like the best. Mediator #1 asks Student #1 which idea he or she thinks will solve the problem. Mediator #2 asks Student #2 the same.

Note: If the students can't agree on a solution, go back to step 3. Make sure the solution(s) they have chosen are realistic.

Review responses and solutions agreed on.

Step 5. Agree.

Ask if this problem/conflict is solved?

Have the students fill out the agreement section of the *Mediator's Report Form* on page 67.

Ask what they could do to prevent this from happening again. Congratulate the students on solving *their* problem. Ask them to only tell their friends that the problem has been solved. Thank them for coming and trying mediation.

Note: If students continue to break the rules or can not solve the conflict, refer the situation back to an administrator, counselor, or advisor.

Mediator's Report Form

Mediators: _____   _____

                                            Date _____

Names of the Students in Conflict   _____

_____

What type of conflict?   _____ Argument   _____ Friendship

                              _____ Fight   _____ Property

                              _____ Rumor   _____ Threat

                              _____ Other _____

Who decided this conflict needed mediating?   ____ Student   ____ Administrator

       ____ Teacher   ____ Assistant   ____ Counselor   ____ Yourself

What was the conflict about? _____

_____

Was the conflict resolved in mediation?   _____ Yes   _____ No

Agreement Form:

Student _____ agrees	Student _____ agrees
Present	Present
_____	_____
_____	_____
_____	_____
Future	Future
_____	_____
_____	_____
Student's Signature _____	Student's Signature _____

Rules for Mediation

1. Agree you want to solve the problem/conflict.

2. Be honest.

3. Treat each other with respect.

4. Listen to each other with an open mind without interrupting.

5. Agree to come up with ways to solve the problem/conflict.

6. Agree to carry out your agreement for solving the problem/conflict.

7. Do not discuss this situation with friends after you leave mediation.

Role of *Peace Patrols*

Problem should be solved with your *head* and *heart*, and not your *hand*.

What does a Peace Patrol do?

Chris Gervais

1. Serve as a peer model.

2. Keep an eye out for any problems that might be considered bullying.

3. If an argument arises:

    Identify yourself.

    Ask the people to use soft voices.

    Listen to both sides.

    Ask each person what it is that he or she wants the other person to stop doing.

    Ask each person if he or she is able to stop doing these things.

    Ask the students to apologize and shake hands.

    Ask students if the problem is solved or if it should be referred to the teacher/counselor.

    If the problem has not been solved, take it to an adult.

What a Peace Patrol does not do:

1. Scold or demand
2. Pass judgments
3. Force themselves on others

Peace Patrols will be:

1. On school busses—like flight attendants, they will welcome students on the bus and help the bus driver form a positive atmosphere.
2. In the cafeteria—at breakfast and lunch.
3. In hallways and restrooms.

    The Peace Patrol will have positive slips to give out to students for a job well done.

    Example: Thanks for keeping the Peace.

Videos:

Peer Mediation—Student Workshop: Sunburst 800-431-1934

Student Watch—Winthrop University 803-323-4740

Conflict Manager's Commitment

I will:

1. Behave responsibly.
2. Be fair and honest.
3. Keep information confidential.
4. Complete the *Mediator's Report Form* accurately.
5. Return to class immediately after mediation.
6. Make up classwork.
7. Be a Peer Mediator or Peace Patrol until the end of the school year.

Student Signature _____   Date _____

Teacher Signature _____   Date _____

Parent Signature _____   Date _____

Certificate
of
Completion

_____

Has Successfully Completed

Leadership Training in
Conflict Management Skills

at

_____

School

_____

Director's Signature

2. Intervention Tools

A Healthy Self-Esteem

A healthy self-esteem is a personal characteristic which is shaped by cultural traditions and social institutions such as families and schools. Therefore, family and school environments play an important part in enhancing self-esteem. Here is some information and ideas.

Having a healthy self-esteem places a child in a much less vulnerable position to become a bully or be victimized. Along with a healthy self-esteem comes a feeling of peace and well being. These individuals are more able to make good choices, be true friends, and demonstrate positive leadership skills.

Educational literature emphasizes the importance of resilient behavior as it relates to school success and a healthy self-esteem. Part of mastering resiliency is taking part in opportunities that allow us to come back. Successful resiliency is a reinforcing behavior. When given opportunities to prove you can succeed under adverse conditions, your self-esteem grows and you internalize the ability to feel in control throughout life.

There are five important components to a healthy self-esteem:

1. A feeling of security (at home, at school, and in the neighborhood)
2. A positive identity (feeling noticed for one's strengths and for doing what is expected)
3. A feeling of belonging (emotional link to home and/or school)
4. A sense of purpose (meaningful goals have been identified)
5. A feeling of competence (being good at something one enjoys)

Parents and school personnel can help children develop a healthy self-esteem. Adults should:

1. Set and communicate high expectations.
2. Give caring and insightful feedback.
3. Encourage youngsters to be involved in at least one school/community event (athletic team, club, community service project, or church fellowship group.)
4. Help children achieve mastery in something they choose.
5. Set up opportunities for children to give of themselves to others or a cause.
6. Practice good decision making skills and independent work habits.
7. Establish a personal faith and respect in something greater than oneself.

8. Allow youngsters to be in situations that are challenging enough to fail. If we always protect our children from disappointment, they will remain confident only under ideal conditions. When life hands out adverse conditions, which will happen, they will be inadequately prepared to cope.

9. Give thought to your own adult modeling behavior at times of adversity. Share how you cope when times are tough, and use those moments as "teachable moments." Let children understand the process you use to make "lemonade out of lemons."

Parents can contribute to a healthy self-esteem. Six factors have been identified as common family influences in homes of bullies. Parents can help build a healthy self-esteem by eliminating the influences found in *Homes of Bullies* and providing the influences found in *Homes Contributing to a Healthy Self-Esteem.*

Family Influences	
Homes Contributing to a Healthy Self-Esteem	**Homes of Bullies**
Warm and inviting atmosphere	Rejection and negativism
Monitor children's whereabouts	Permissiveness and aggression
Aggressive behavior is not considered acceptable	Parental aggression
Fair and consistent discipline	Inconsistent discipline
Monitor television, movie viewing, music, friends, and so forth	Lack of monitoring (TV, movies, friends, music, videos and so forth)
Family talk time is practiced	Lack of strategies for solving family problems

What Should Parents Do to Help Decrease Bullying?

1. Listen, ask, and talk about your child's school day.
2. Watch for any changes in behavior that concern you.
3. Reduce or eliminate the amount of television time that involves violence.
4. Clearly communicate to your child that your family does not tolerate behavior that hurts another person.
5. Try avoiding physical punishment in your family. Set clear rules and follow through with consequences such as limiting privileges or using time out.
6. Expect your child's school to have written school rules regarding bullying. Consider serving on a parent committee.
7. Keep a *written record* of your observations concerning your child's behavior. Let the school know immediately if you believe your child has been bullied.
8. Teach and practice specific sentences with your child that can help him or her respond assertively to a bully. For example:
    A. "Thanks, I didn't think you noticed."
    B. "I don't have a problem with that, do you?"
    C. "Leave me alone."

What Should Teachers Do to Help Decrease Bullying?

1. Post the school rules against bullying in the classroom.
2. Post a class pledge. (page 78)
3. Attend to students' behaviors throughout the day (recess, lunch, and restroom time).
4. Consistently intervene in any possible bullying situations by using consequences.
5. Initiate individual talks with bullies to confront them with inappropriate behaviors.
6. Initiate, when necessary, counseling for students with low self-esteem.
7. Use all students to effectively initiate a Peace Patrol Program.
8. Involve parents when appropriate in conferences with students.
9. Help all students assert themselves regarding their emotional, physical, and mental health.
10. Use class meetings to address bullying behavior that occurs in the classroom, school, or on the school grounds, and affects the entire class's ability to learn.
11. Write a newsletter, make a book, or do a skit, about *Getting Equipped To Stop Bullying.*
12. Pair older students with younger students as peer helpers.

Other activities and suggestions for teachers:

1. Class Meetings

Class meetings are an effective way to deal with bullying and gain support and understanding for victims. The meeting should:

1. Start with positives.
2. Identify concerns, focusing on *behavior*, not individuals.
3. Problem solve.
4. End on a positive note.

2. Anger Corners

On a piece of paper have the students make symbols for "Steaming", "Hot," "Lukewarm," and "Cool"; one in each corner of the page. As you read one of the situation cards (Page 46), the student moves a chip, to represent himself or herself, to the appropriate corner of the paper. Have a class discussion about what could be done in that situation. You can make up your own situation cards.

3. Slogan Contest

Have a *calm down* or *cool off* slogan contest.

4. Room Deco

Make a bulletin board or poster with the following reminder:

If someone is bothering you:

1. Stay calm so you can think clearly.
2. Use "I" messages.
3. Ask yourself: What am I letting bother me?

Why do I find it bothersome?

How would I like things to change?

5. How Could the Story End?

Have your students write a portion of a short story about anger on a colored strip of paper:

- The persons with red strips write the beginning of the story describing why they are angry.

- The persons with yellow strips write the middle of the story describing how they can feel less angry.

- The persons with green strips write the end of the story describing a positive ending.

Put the strips together, one of each color, to make a story. You may want to give specific examples for younger children.

What Should Administrators Do to Help Decrease Bullying?

Consider setting up:

1. A variety of school clubs and encourage *all* students to join one (drama, cooking, running, photography, art).

2. Workshop for parents on the importance of getting their children involved.

3. A redesign of the playground to increase chances for participation.

4. A school wide, year long emphasis on peer support and mediation.

5. A variety of community service projects for students.

6. A few minutes of quiet time each day for students to reflect upon the type of person one respects and admires.

7. Soothing music in the school, when and where appropriate.

8. Ways of providing mentors to children who have been identified as a victim or bully.

9. Suggestions for school board members and Business Partners with requests for support. (Finance summer leadership program, clubs, and after school programs.)

10. The strategy of taking a bully aside and telling him or her someone is picking on _____ and needs their help; the bully becomes their guardian.

11. Time to report good news stories over the PA or in the school newspaper.

12. School Intervention Team meetings to define strategies and develop communications among school personnel to decrease bullying.

13. The practice of using letters such as the example on the next page to communicate with parents and assist children in learning choices and consequences.

These are a few examples. List five additional ideas that could contribute to an increase in school connecting:

1. _____

2. _____

3. _____

4. _____

5. _____

Dear Parents,

Today, your child was fighting at school. There are a number of reasons why children choose to fight. It is important to share that it is your child's choice to fight or not to fight and with that choice comes consequences. Help your child understand that no one wins a fight. Fighting is not worth your child's time.

Below, your child has described what happened. Your input is important in helping your child solve or avoid future problems.

Thank you for working together,

Principal __ _____

Dear Mom and Dad,

I am having trouble getting along with other children. Today I fought with_____

I chose to fight because_____

Fighting did not solve the problem. Two choices I can try if this problem happens again:

1.   _____
2.   _____

Please talk with me about other ways to settle disagreements.
This is my _____ (1st, 2nd, 3rd...) fight this year.
The following are consequences for my fighting:

_____
_____
_____

This is not my first fight, so I also have to be:
❏ Referred to the School Intervention Team.
❏ Involved in a conference with my parents, teacher, and principal.
❏ Removed from my classroom for _____ day(s).
❏ Suspended up to _____ school days.
❏ _____.

Signatures:

Child   _____   Parent _____

Teacher   _____   Principal _____

Conference Date _____   Location _____

Class Pledge

1. We shall not bully others by physical contact, verbal comments, gestures, or isolation.

2. We shall try to help students who are bullied.

3. We will include students who are left out.

Becki Boatwright, Ph.D., LPC; Teresea Mathis, Ed.S, LMSW; and Susan Smith-Rex, Ed.D.

OTHER RESOURCES

CHILDRENS BOOKS:

(K-3)

Bosch, C. (1988). *Bully on the bus.* Seattle, WA: Parenting Press.

Carlson, N. (1988). *I like me.* New York, NY; Viking

Cole, J. (1988). *The missing tooth.* New York, NY: Random House.

Crary, E. (1994). *I'm furious.* Seattle, WA: Parenting Press.

Crary, E. (1992). *I'm mad.* Seattle, WA: Parenting Press.

Douglass, B. (1988). *Good news.* New York, NY: Lothrop, Lee, and Shepard.

Duncan, R. (1989). *When Emily woke up angry.* New York, NY: Barron's Ed Services.

Everitt, B. (1995). *Mean soup.* San Francisco, CA: HarBarce

Gambill, H. (1982). *Self-control.* Elgin, IL: The Child's World.

Grunsell, A. (1989). *Bullying.* New York, NY: Glouster Press.

Hogan, P. (1980). *Sometimes I get so mad.* Chatham, NJ: Raintree Steck-V.

Isenberg, B. (1987). *Albert the Running Bear gets the jitters.* New York, NY: Clarion.

Jones, R. (1991). *Matthew and Tilly.* New York, NY: Dutton.

Moser, A. (1994). *Don't rant and rave on Wednesdays!* Kansas City, MO: Landmark Edns.

Simon, Norma. (1974). *I'm so mad.* Morton Grove, IL: Whitman.

Wade, B. (1990). *Little monsters.* New York, NY: Lothrop, Lee, and Shepard.

Whitehouse, E. & Pudney, W. (1996). *A volcano in my tummy.* Cabriola, Canada: New Society.

Winthrop, E. (1990). *Luke's bully.* New York, NY: Viking.

(4-6)

Carrick, C. (1976). *Accident.* New York, NY: Houghton-Mifflin.

Grimes, N. (1994). *Meet Danitra Brown.* New York, NY: Lothrop, Lee, and Shepard.

Hooper, NJ. (1984). *Ape, Ears and Beaky.* New York, NY: Dutton,

Roberta, B. (1993). *Sticks and stones, Bobbie Bones.* New York, NY: Scholastic.

VIDEOS:

(K-3)

Handling Emotions. (Film Ideas 800-475-3456).

I get so mad. (Sunburst 800-431-1934).

I'm so Frustrated. (Sunburst 800-431-1934).

No one quite like me or you. (Sunburst 800-431-1934).

Stressbusters. (Sunburst 800-431-1934).

(4-6)

Be Cool. (James Stanfield 800-421-6534).

Broken toy. (The Summerhills Group 614-455-2035).

Don't pick on me. (Sunburst 800-431-1934).

Martin meets the pirates. (Altschul 800-421-2363).

Settling Disagreements, Disputes, and Fights. (Learning Tree 303-740-9777).

Skate expectations. (Focus on the Family 800-932-9123).

Solving Conflicts. (Winthrop University 803-323-4047).

Stress and You. (Sunburst 800-431-1934).

When You are Mad, Mad, Mad: Dealing with Anger. (Sunburst 800-431-1934).

FOR HELP:

Center to Prevent Handgun Violence, 1225 I Street, Suite 1100, NW, Washington, DC 2005; 202-289-7319.

Children's Creative Response to Conflict (CCRC). Box 271, 523 North Broadway, Nyack, NY 10960; 914-358-4601.

Family Research Institute, University of New Hampshire, 128 Horton Social Science Center, Durham, NH 03824; 603-862-2761.

Family Violence & Sexual Assault Institute, 1310 Clinic Drive, Tyler, TX 75701; 903-595-6600.

Johnson Institute, 7205 Ohms Lane, Minneapolis, MN 55439-2159; 612-831-1630.

National Center on Child Abuse and Neglect, P.O. Box 1182, Washington, DC 20013-1182; 703-385-7565.

National Criminal Justice Reference Service, 1600 Research Boulevard, Rockville, MD 20850; 800 051-3420.

National School Safety Center, Pepperdine University. Malibu, CA 90263; 818-377-6200.

REFERENCES

Chandler, K., Chapman, C., Rand, M. & Taylor, B. (1998). *Students' reports of school crime: 1989 and 1995.* Washington, DC: U. S. Departments of Education and Justice.

ERIC Digest. (1997 Aug/Sept). *Education Week.*

Frank, K. & Smith, S. (1994). *Getting a grip on ADD: A kid's guide to understanding and coping with attention disorders.* Minneapolis, MN: Educational Media Corporation.

Frank, K. & Smith-Rex, S. (1995). *Getting a life of your own: A kid's guide to understanding and coping with family alcoholism.* Minneapolis, MN: Educational Media Corporation.

Frank, K. & Smith-Rex, S. (1996). *Getting over the blues: A kids guide to understanding and coping with unpleasant feelings and depression.* Minneapolis, MN: Educational Media Corporation.

Frank, K. & Smith-Rex, S. (1997). *Getting with it: A kid's guide to forming good relationships and fitting in.* Minneapolis, MN: Educational Media Corporation.

Olweus, D. Schoolyard bullying-grounds for intervention. *School Safety,* Fall 1987, pp.26-27.

Smith, S. (1992, Sept). How to decrease bullying in our schools. *Principal,* Vol. 72.

Smith, S. & Walter, G. (1988). *Four steps to making friends.* Rock Hill, SC: Winthrop University.

Stanfield, J. (1992). *Be Cool Series: Coping with difficult people.* Santa Barbara, CA: James Stanfield. 800-421-6534.

Time, May 18, 1998.

U. S. Department of Education. (1998). *Violence and discipline problems in U. S. public schools: 1996-97.* National Center for Educational Statistics; NCES 98-030.